POEMS FOR
CHILDREN BY

ANNIE M. G. SCHMIDT

PINK LEMONADE

TRANSLATED AND ADAPTED FROM THE DUTCH BY

HENRIETTA
TEN HARMSEL

ILLUSTRATED
BY
LINDA CARES

PUBLISHED BY
WM. B. EERDMANS

Copyright © 1981 by Wm. B. Eerdmans Publishing Company
255 Jefferson Ave., S.E., Grand Rapids, Michigan 49503
Illustrations Copyright © 1981 by Linda Cares

Translated from the Dutch by arrangement with Annie M. G. Schmidt and Em. Querido's Uitgeverij B. V., Amsterdam, from the following books: *De lapjeskat, De toren van Bemmelekom, Ik ben lekker stout, Op visite bij de reus, Iedereen heeft een staart, De graaf van Weet ik veel, Veertien uilen, Het fluitketeltje, Dag, meneer de kruidenier, Niet met de deuren slaan.*

Copyright © 1950, 1952, 1954, 1955, 1956, 1957, 1959, 1960, 1973 by Annie M. G. Schmidt.

Library of Congress Cataloging in Publication Data

Schmidt, Annie M. G.
Pink lemonade.

Summary: An illustrated collection of more than forty poems which include characters such as Miss Lickapan, Isabelle Caramella and her white cat, and a pig that wanted a career.
[1. Dutch poetry] 1. Harmsel, Henrietta ten.
II. Cares, Linda, ill. III. Title.
PT5868.S313P5 839.3′1164 81-5591
ISBN 0-8028-4050-7 AACR2

TABLE OF CONTENTS

Pink Lemonade 4

Nothing at All 6

Chicky-Chick 8

Henry John and Henry Joe 10

The Pig 11

The Bad Bee 12

Lazy Little Lickerfun 13

The Robbers and the Moon 14

The Furniture 16

Weeping Willie 17

The Fly Lily Jo 18

The Nice Fat Lady 20

The Little Bed That Can Ride 22

On the Farm 24

Little Miss Lickapan 26

Isabella Caramella 28

Flopsy's New Suit 30

Miss Poker 32

Counting in Rhyme 33

No Steps 34

The Girl with Nylon Hair 35

Doll Party 36

The Lady of Castle Van Karp 38

Electric Blanket 40

The Magic Wand 42

Circus Song 44

Summer Evening 45

What is That, Mrs. Van Teller? 46

On the Green 48

Late at Night 49

The Goat of Dr. Pottle 50

Johanna Cracklebone 51

Henderson of Lexington 52

The Best Child 54

Is Kittily-Puss a Cat? 55

The Ducks 56

Calm, Calm 57

The Clean Queen 58

A-Nibble No, A-Nibble Nice 59

The Proud Little Light 60

The Cuckoo Theodore 62

The Time of Elves 64

In a beautiful garden in faraway France
    Cool paths curve along in the shade,
And tulips and lilies and roses surround
    A pond full of pink lemonade.

The children go rowing around in a boat —
    It's never against the law —
And when they're not singing, they take a cool sip
    Through a very long, elegant straw.

The pond is bright pink, almost raspberry red,
    And sometimes the children may wade
With trousers and dresses pulled up very high
    In the pond full of pink lemonade.

If one of the children flops out of the boat,
    They rescue him quick as a wink,
And then they start licking so that he won't stay
    So terribly sticky and pink!

It really is charming, that garden in France —
    The flowers, the paths in the shade —
But still you'll agree that the nicest of all
    Is the pond full of pink lemonade.

PINK
LEMONADE

Nothing at All

Three little mice and a big, tall giraffe
Walked toward the village, a mile and a half.
When they had come to a beautiful wall,
All the mice stopped and said, "Isn't it tall?
What could be back there? We can't figure out!
Roses, and tulips, and daisies, no doubt.
Mr. Giraffe, won't you please take a look?
What is it like? Like a fairy-tale book?"
So the giraffe turned his long neck around,
Tilted his head to gaze down at the ground.

For a long time he looked over the wall;
Then he said, "Sorry, there's nothing at all."

Three little mice and a big, tall giraffe
Went right on walking a mile and a half.
When they came up to a very high hedge,
All the mice tried to look over the edge:
"Since we're too small, and the hedge is too high,
Mr. Giraffe, will you give it a try?
There must be beautiful things to be seen;
Maybe the house of a king or a queen.
Surely some elves or some fairies live there."
So the giraffe turned and started to stare,
Stood on his toes, but he soon gave a call,
"No, it's too bad, but there's nothing at all."

So it went on, and at first it seemed sad;
Later, however, the mice got quite mad!
After conferring, they made up their mind
To leave this silly giraffe behind.
So the three mice, with a giggle and laugh,
Walked on alone for a mile and a half.
Now as they walk by that wall every day,
You should just hear what those little mice say:
"This is the house of the king and the queen!
Back of this wall there is much to be seen —
Dragons, and flowers, and a bear in his den —"
Since they believe it, they're happy again.

But the giraffe, he stayed sadly behind;
He is so tall that he can't change his mind.
So every time he looks over a wall,
He still says, "Really, there's nothing at all."

Chicky-Chick

"Look here," a rooster called one day,
"Listen what I have to say!
Here's a colored egg — you see?
On the grass right next to me.
Did you lay it, Chicky Chick?
If you did, just tell me quick."

Poor Chicky blushed and scratched her head:
"It really wasn't hard," she said.
"While waiting for that egg to come,
I dreamed about an Easter poem,
And as the dream began to fade —
KERFLOP! That pretty egg was laid
With flowers and bunnies on the shell.
Don't you think I did quite well?"

"Oh, fooey," said the cock, "you would!
Such an egg is just no good.
Chicken eggs are always white;
All those colors are a fright!"
The angry cackling hens agreed:
"An Easter egg! Pooh pooh! Indeed!
Away," they clucked, right to her face,
"Go lay your eggs some other place.
Just find some other neighborhood."
So Chicky had to leave for good.

There she walked across the green,
Saddest hen you've ever seen,
And after days of wandering,
She reached the palace of the king.
"That's the place for me to stop!
I'm so tired that I could drop.
Perhaps they'll help me if I beg —"
When OOPS, she laid an Easter egg!

The king had never, never seen
Such an egg of blue and green.
He ordered, "Bring that chick to me
And treat her very courteously."
She ate a royal worm and then
The people called her QUITE A HEN!
She got a royal Leghorn band,
And now she's known throughout the land.

She now has grand associates
And eats her grain from golden plates.
She has her morning toast and tea
Beside his Royal Majesty!
And for Prince John and Princess May
She lays a colored egg each day.

9

Henry John and Henry Joe

There was a pair of little boys
    down in New Mexico,
The first one's name was Henry John,
    the other's Henry Joe.
They were exactly even old —
    they looked just like their mother —
In fact, they looked exact-exact-
    exactly like each other.
And if you'd say, "Hi, Henry John,"
    then he would answer, "No,
My brother's name is Henry John,
    but I am Henry Joe."

Their father couldn't even tell
    exactly who was who;
If he would say, "Now Henry Joe
    stop all that hullabaloo,"
Then Henry Joe would answer him,
    "Why, Pop, I'm not the one,
You thought that it was Henry Joe,
    but it was Henry John."
When Henry John got in a mess,
    his brother, Henry Joe,
Would get the blame, and even worse,
    he also got the blow.

"Now who is who?" their father said;
    "now who is really who?"
Or is it just the best for me
    to spank each one of you?
I cannot keep you two apart,
    and neither can your mother,
For each of you looks just exact-
    exactly like his brother!"
He grabbed the scissors, grabbed one boy,
    and cut off all his hair!
His head looked like a bowling ball,
    so shiny and so bare.

The other boy was forced to wear
    two braids upon his head!
"All right, from now on I will know
    who's who," the father said.
But look, the poor man still can't tell;
    "I'll be! I still don't know!
The bald one, is that Henry John,
    or is it Henry Joe?"
And so the father still repeats
    just as he used to do:
"Now which is which, and what is what,
    and who is really who?"

The Pig

There once was a pig who lived out on a farm
    Who wanted to be something great;
His brothers and sisters were quite satisfied
    To grunt and to simply gain weight.
But this little pig said, "Oh, no," and "Oh, dear!
I want to be different, I want a career."

So he got a job in an office downtown:
    He typed, and he opened the mail,
He sorted the letters and answered the phone,
    And he served all the rich clientele;
His telephone manners were splendid: "Hello. . .
Yes, this is the piggy at Bartels and Co."

The boss at the office said, "Look at that pig!
    We're lucky to have him, I'm sure.
He's better at typing than anyone else
    We've had at this office before.
That first little typist we had was too slow,
    The second one terribly lazy,
But this little pig is the best that we've had:
    Just look at him working like crazy.
Yes, if this continues from April through May,
We surely will give him a raise in his pay."

At quarter past five, without making a fuss,
The pig locks the doors and goes home on the bus,
And says as he sits with his mother at tea,
"That job really has been the making of me."

The Bad Bee

A bee — now don't be frightened, dears —
Had buzzed around for many years

And said, "Now that I've made a study,
I think I'll go and sting somebody.

Right in the nose would suit me best,
That spot has caught my interest."

But the right spot was hard to find,
For noses come in many a kind!

He saw such noses on the street!
Some red, some ugly, and some sweet.

Just when the right one caught his eye,
He'd see a better one nearby.

"Right there," he'd say, "my stinger goes!"
But then he'd see a fatter nose.

And when he heard the curfew ring,
He hadn't found a nose to sting.

By then all noses had gone in,
Each one asleep with its own chin!

The bee flew home to his own place
With big tears running down his face.

And there his mother heard him say,
"Mama, this

       just

          was

             not

                my

                   day!"

Lazy Little Lickerfun

Four little pigs in Peru.
What do they do? What do they do?
They prune the trees,
and tend the bees.
They work very hard
to clean the yard.
They hoe and weed
and plant the seed.
They run machines
and pick the beans.
They do everything that has to be done,
that is — all four little pigs but one —
that lazy lazy little one,
that lazy little Lickerfun.

Four little pigs in Peru.
But what does Lickerfun do?
"Oh," they say,
"He will not paint,
for he's too faint!
He will not mow,
He feels too low.
To cook or bake
would make him ache.
To hew or hack
would hurt his back.
He sleeps from dawn to setting sun —
that lazy little Lickerfun."

But then at the end of the day
when the pigs put their work away,
then out comes lazy Lickerfun
as soon as all the work is done:
"Now I'll just eat some turnips, too!"
But all of his brothers shout, "Not you!
Not work, but eat?" they say,
    "Like fun!"
Oh! Oh! Now nothing can be done
for lazy little Lickerfun.

The Robbers and the Moon

Far, far away in Italy three robbers had a den;
It wasn't very pleasant — they were really horrid men!
Their den was far too crowded, it was filled with all their loot;
Their silver and their diamonds and four tons of gold to boot.
They sat among their treasures saying, "This is quite a deal!
We want to go out robbing, but we don't know what to steal."
They thought of all the fancy things, the elegant, the pretty,
But they had stolen every-every-everything already.

Their den was very dark, but through a crack they saw the moon,
A smiling, full, luxurious one — it was the month of June.
"The moon! Why, that's a good idea! That's just what we will steal!
Come on," they said, "let's go up there and see how that will feel!"
They took the tower of Pisa, one from Florence, and one from Rome
And piled them on each other — higher than the highest dome.
They started up, and though they felt a little dizzy soon,
They shouted happily, "We're off! We're off to rob the moon!"

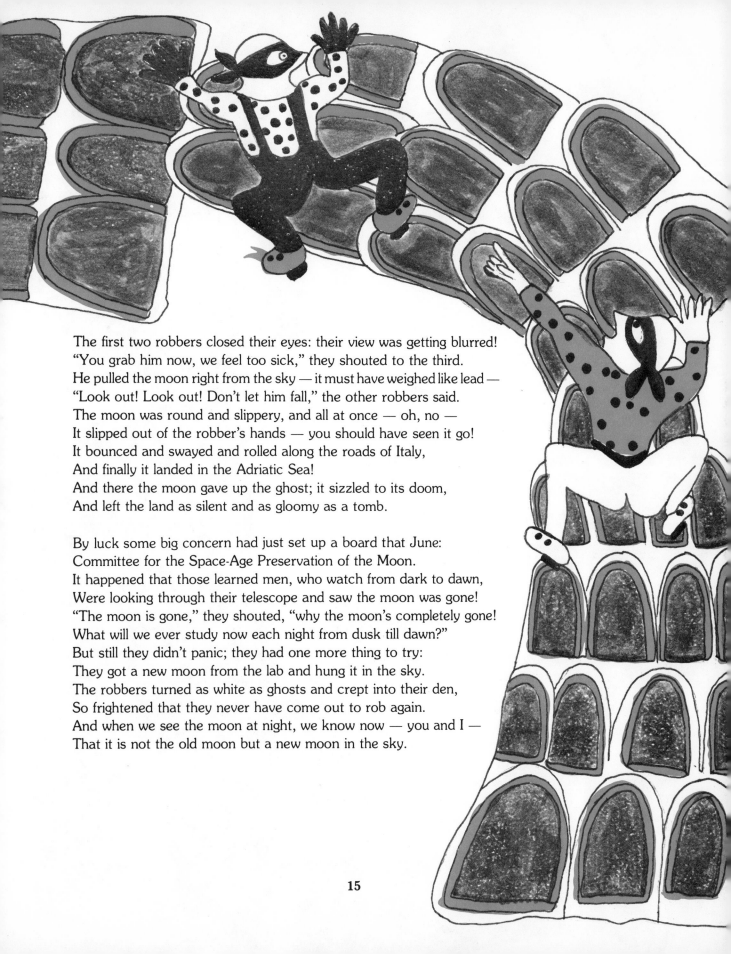

The first two robbers closed their eyes: their view was getting blurred!
"You grab him now, we feel too sick," they shouted to the third.
He pulled the moon right from the sky — it must have weighed like lead —
"Look out! Look out! Don't let him fall," the other robbers said.
The moon was round and slippery, and all at once — oh, no —
It slipped out of the robber's hands — you should have seen it go!
It bounced and swayed and rolled along the roads of Italy,
And finally it landed in the Adriatic Sea!
And there the moon gave up the ghost; it sizzled to its doom,
And left the land as silent and as gloomy as a tomb.

By luck some big concern had just set up a board that June:
Committee for the Space-Age Preservation of the Moon.
It happened that those learned men, who watch from dark to dawn,
Were looking through their telescope and saw the moon was gone!
"The moon is gone," they shouted, "why the moon's completely gone!
What will we ever study now each night from dusk till dawn?"
But still they didn't panic; they had one more thing to try:
They got a new moon from the lab and hung it in the sky.
The robbers turned as white as ghosts and crept into their den,
So frightened that they never have come out to rob again.
And when we see the moon at night, we know now — you and I —
That it is not the old moon but a new moon in the sky.

The Furniture

"How would you like to take a walk?"
The table asked the chair,
"I get so stiff of standing still,
Let's take a stroll out there."
"A walk sounds lovely," said the chair,
"This room is quite a bore;
We have four legs, and — after all —
That's what our legs are for."

"Please, may I go along with you?"
Inquired the big buffet.
"I'm very heavy, so I'll walk
Quite slowly, if I may:
I have my stomach full of plates
And glasses, as you know."
And then he asked the bookcase,
And she said, "I'd love to go."

So they went walking in the park
To see the flowers bloom,
But Mr. Clock and Mr. Lamp—
They mightn't leave the room.
They mumbled and they grumbled,
But they weren't allowed to roam,
For that's the way it is:
The ones who don't have legs stay home.

Weeping Willie

This is the song of Weeping Will,
Who cried and cried all day.
Weeping Willie would cry and cry —
He never knew exactly why —
He cried for years, they say.

His tears would trickle on the floor
A-drip, a-drip, a-drop,
And then the maid would come around
And wipe them with her mop.

Every morning for years and years
Willie sat down to eat,
But when he'd hardly eaten yet
The tablecloth was soaking wet
With Weeping Willie's tears.

His tears would fall upon his plate
And overflow his cup,
And then the maid would come again
To wipe the business up.

But one day Weeping Willie's maid
Decided to leave town;
His tears were soon too much for him:
He tried to float, he tried to swim,
He thought for sure he'd drown.

And after that poor Weeping Will
Was never, never found,
Though no one absolutely proved
That he was really drowned.

But when I hear some little child
Who's crying BOO HOO HOO,
I think, "There's Weeping Willie —
Or was it maybe *you*?"

17

The Fly Lily Jo

Down south in sunny Mexico
There lived a fly named Lily Jo.
The prettiest fly in all the land —
Delightful, elegant, and grand.

Out on the pleasant balcony
She buzzed around her cup of tea.
And down below, perched on a flower,
A horsefly watched her hour by hour.
His coat was green and blue — like fur —
He hoped that he could marry her,
For he had lived alone too long;
So now he hummed this little song:

But Lily Jo stuck to her tea,
For she was very proud, you see;
Last Sunday, near her uncle's farm,
She bit a Spaniard in the arm.
And so she bragged: "Tra la la lee,
I now have Spanish blood in me.
A horsefly? That would never do;
No, I can never marry you!"
But still he sat there on his flower
And kept on singing, hour by hour:

Oh, Lily Jo, oh, Lily Jo,
The sweetest fly in Mexico,
Please say that you will marry me;
Just think how happy we would be!
Oh, Lily Jo, oh, Lily Jo,
The sweetest fly in Mexico.

And now the horsefly at her door
Sings just as sadly as before:
"She is the one I still prefer,
And she had Spanish blood in her!"

Oh, Lily Jo, oh, Lily Jo,
The sweetest fly in Mexico,
If only she had married me,
Just think how happy we would be!
Oh, Lily Jo, oh, Lily Jo,
The sweetest fly in Mexico.

Oh, Lily Jo, oh, Lily Jo,
The sweetest fly in Mexico,
Please say that you will marry me;
Just think how happy we would be!
Oh, Lily Jo, oh, Lily Jo,
The sweetest fly in Mexico.

But Lily Jo was now so proud
Her head was nearly in a cloud.
And since her nose was in the air,
She didn't see the swallow there.
He zoomed straight down and then — oh, no —
He swallowed up poor Lily Jo!

The Nice Fat Lady

A nice fat lady in St. Paul
Baked cookies every day.
She baked and baked, pan after pan,
And gave them all away.
Her relatives, her visitors,
The children on her street
All thought her cookies were so good
They'd eat and eat and eat.
But when they said, "Now that's enough;
We've eaten all we can,"
She wouldn't stop because she still
Had batter in her pan.

The friends who came to visit her
Went staggering down the street;
Her cat looked like a cannon ball —
He had so much to eat.
Her dog and all her neighbor's dogs
Got bigger, rounder, fatter,
But yet she said she couldn't stop
Because she still had batter!

The teacher from the school next door
Brought all his pupils out
To see why people looked so round —
What made them groan and shout.
But when they saw the cookies there,
They all began to eat,
And soon they went a-groaning and
A-moaning down the street.

20

And when the neighbors shouted, "Stop!
This is a serious matter!"
The lady said, "I cannot stop
Because I still have batter."

The people from the factories —
Their bosses, too, it seems —
Fell down in rows along the walk,
All bursting at the seams.
Although the people got so fat
That they began to roll,
She wouldn't stop because she still
Had batter in her bowl.

But finally the people said,
"We can't eat any more."
So then she piled the cookies up
In baskets on the floor.
She filled the houses and the barns,
And in the city square
She piled up cookies till they made
A mountain in the air!
Alas! The mountain fell apart —
It made a noise like thunder;
And as it fell, the lady was
Completely buried under!
Just as she disappeared and heard
The cookie-thunder roll,
She said, "Oh, dear, and I still had
Some batter in my bowl."

There's still one thing I have to say
Before this story ends:
If you decide that you will bake
Some cookies for your friends,
Just think this over carefully —
It's an important matter:
It's dangerous to make too much
Delicious cookie batter.

The Little Bed That Can Ride

Well, well, what do you say?
John has a bed that can ride away.
Every night, in his white PJ's
He pulls up his knee,
He turns the key,
He says "So long" to the sheep on the wall,
And there goes his bed right down the hall.

Quick and neat
Down the street
Through the dark he drives his bed,
With great care
Through the square
Stoplights flashing green and red.
Toot, toot, toot! Beep, beep, beep!
Johnny rides while others sleep.

His bed goes fast, terribly fast!
Look at the cars,
        the trucks,
        the bikes!
Just as busy as Johnny likes!
First through a tunnel —
A bridge — and then
He rides to New York
And back again.

Then into his room — quick as a leap —
For Johnny is tired
And wants to sleep.
He says "Good night" to the sheep on the wall,
And falls asleep curled up like a ball.
Next morning his mom says, "Where have you been?"
"The same," says John, "to New York again."

23

On the Farm

When the farmer and his wife go on vacation,
All the animals show great cooperation.
They all line up in a hurry,
And they say, "Now don't you worry,
We'll take care of everything."
The horse says he
will set the tea,
and the cat
will clean the mat,
and the parrots
cook the carrots
in the pan.
"All of us," they say, "will do the best we can."

When the farmer and his wife get
        in the car,
Right away the chickens fetch the
        pail of tar
And they tar the windows tight

24

while the dog
holds the pail
with his tail.
All the ponies
rake the hay
in the field
across the way.
How those animals are working night and day.

When the farmer and his wife are at the
     park,
All the rabbits work like mad
     from dawn to dark.
Every rabbit
has the habit
of polishing
the floor.
And the goat
wears a coat
as he opens
the front door.
And a lamb
makes the jam,
while the kittens
knit the mittens.
As they work they say, "Well, you
     can bet your life
That this will please the farmer
     and his wife."

When the farmer and his wife come back to see,
     Everything
Is just as nice
     just as nice
     just as nice
          as it can be!

Little Miss Lickapan

There once was a land with a princess, I'm told,
Who wore little gloves and a dress spun of gold.
Her shoes were of silver, she carried a fan,
And the name of this princess was Miss Lickapan.
A princess named Lickapan? How can that be?
She always was snooping and nibbling, you see.
She snooped the bananas, the cookies, the rolls;
She licked all the pans, and she licked all the bowls.
She always was licking, that's why they began
To give her the name Little Miss Lickapan.

One bright Easter morning she opened her eyes
At quarter past six, so she thought she'd arise.
The birds were all singing — all in a gay mood —
But Little Miss Lickapan only smelled food.
The flowers looked nice, but she hurried to see
What the cook had prepared for the King's royal tea.
She went to the kitchen; she loved the good smell
Of frosting and almonds and pie in the shell.
She sniffed at the soup and at all the good things
That cooks always make every Easter for kings.

Not a sound to be heard, just the clock ticking slow —
But there on the floor stood a huge tub of dough.
"Just one little sample to taste what's in there,"
Said Miss Lickapan — but then, oh, what a scare!
The princess fell into the tub — oh, oh, oh!
She fell with a splash in the Easter-cake dough!
Her father and mother, who loved to sleep late,
Didn't come down the stairs until quarter past eight.
But soon they got worried, for no one could see
Their Little Miss Lickapan — where could she be?

26

They all started looking — they hunted like mad —
In corners, in closets, and under the bed.
They searched all the gardens till quarter to three,
But then it was time for the King's Easter tea.
In came all the guests, at least fourteen fat earls
And ten baronesses with beautiful curls.
They first ate the soup, then some fish from the lake,
Then out came the cook with the big Easter cake.
The poor queen was crying behind her lace fan,
"Oh, dear, what's become of my poor Lickapan?"

"Come on," the King shouted, "just hand me the knife;
You always love Easter cake, dear little wife."
So the King took the knife, and he stuck it in deep,
But, oh, what a shock: The cake started to weep!
The cake gave a howl, the cake gave a shout,
And everyone heard it: "Oh, please let me out."
The King cut in farther — and what do you think?
A big stream of tears came out, frosted in pink.
And then came a foot that was kicking like mad,
And then came the princess, quite sticky, but glad.

Then all round the table the guests said, "My land!"
As Little Miss Lickapan gave them her hand.
"All right!" said the King. "That's enough!" said the Queen.
"Now you just get busy and lick yourself clean."

27

Isabella Caramella

Isabella
Caramella
puts her dolly in the bath.
Isabella
Caramella
has a white woolen cat
and a white woolen mouse and a red-cheeked bunny
and she has a crocodile, she calls him Honey.
Isabella
Caramella
plays so sweetly in the sand.
Isabella
Caramella
with a posy in her hand.

But as soon as big bad people come to visit for a while,
she calls softly "Honey, Honey" to her crocodile.
And like an angry pup
he eats the people up
from their toes to their hair he eats them up:
    GLUP, GLUP.
Like that Madam Kickertoes who never did like girls and boys
and that lady with the scarf who always frowns and can't stand noise
and the crocodile just swallows Mr. Tops right off the lawn
down to the very bottom of the trousers he has on.

        "Isabella
        Caramella
        where is Madam Kickertoes?
        And Mr. Tops and his nice trousers,
        where are they do you suppose?
        And that lady with the scarf,
        did you maybe see her go?"
        Isabella
        Caramella
        simply says, WHY NO!

        And she sits there smiling sweetly
        with her red-cheeked bunny
        and right with her on the doorstep
        sits her crocodile Honey.

        Isabella
        Caramella
        puts her dolly in the bath.
        Isabella
        Caramella
        goes awalking down the path.

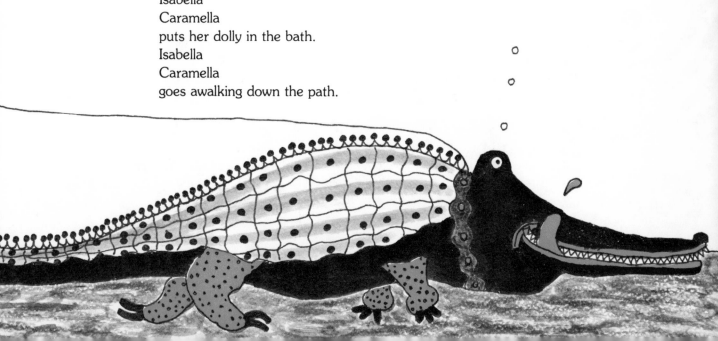

Flopsy's New Suit

Children, I'm sure you know I'm right —
Zebras are always black and white.
Every zebra, as everyone knows,
Has stripes of black on all his clothes.

What's the matter? You think I'm mad?
My word! There stands a zebra in plaid!
There he stands in a checkered suit,
But that one is a funny brute:
      HIS NAME IS FLOP!

When Flop was young, he was just like others;
He was striped like all his zebra brothers.
But one day little Flopsy said,
"I'd like to wear something else instead.
Mother, please give me another suit,
Maybe with flowers — that would be cute —
Or one with figures or other things,
Or rabbits, or bears, or just plain rings."

"No," said his mother, "not at all!
You'd look like wallpaper on the wall.
Stripes, I say, are always right:
White with black and black with white.

Always stripes," his mother said;
"Stripes! Just get that through your head!"

So Flop decided to run away;
He ran and he ran and he ran all day.
Flopsy was gone! How very sad!
But then he came back with a suit of plaid.

"Plaid!" said his father. "That just won't do!
We'll wash that plaid right off of you."
"No," said his mother, "that would be bad;
The stripes would wash away with the plaid.

Then Flop would be completely bare!
I'm sure he'd die of shame, so there!
This is the way we'll fix this botch:
We'll tell our friends that Flop is Scotch!"

Then came the next big zebra day;
All the zebras came over to play.
Flop danced for hours without a stop,
But now his name is new: Mac Flop!

Miss Poker

"Miss Poker, Miss Poker," said Mr. Tong,
"We're hanging here next to the fire.
We've known each other for such a long time,
I now can say, 'I think you're sublime,
You're the one I love and admire.' "

"Why my dear Mr. Tong, my dear Mr. Tong,
I'll marry you right away,
For I'm made of iron and you are, too.
I'll go through smoke and fire with you!
We'll belong to each other for aye!"

Then they danced together, a merry round,
A sarabande by the fire.
The chorus of coals sang a happy song,
And the hanging kettle went ding-a-ding-dong,
And the flames burned higher and higher.

So the Poker and Tong got married last week.
Now they're hanging together, cheek to cheek.
They cuddle each other in all kinds of weather,
And whenever they glow, they glow together.

Counting in Rhyme

Ten little lemon drops in a long line,
One rolled away, and then there were _____
Nine little lemon drops, but in came Auntie Kate;
She took the very biggest one; then there were _____
Eight little lemon drops; along came greedy Marie,
She quickly picked up five of them: Then there were _____

Three lonely lemon drops. But at the corner store
The clerk gave me an extra one: Then there were _____
Four lovely lemon drops. In came my Uncle Ben;
He gave me six all for myself! Then there were _____

Ten little lemon drops. I ate them, every one.
And now the fun is over. Now I have none.

No Steps

When Dad woke up one morning,
    He called, "Well, I must say!
Just look at what has happened:
    Our steps have blown away!"

And Mother said, "How awful!
    We can't get out at all!
For our whole outside staircase
    Has blown right off the wall."

The children all came running
    And called, "Hurray, hurray!
No school for us this morning:
    Our steps have blown away."

Then Dad called up his office
    To say, "Inform the boss
I can't come in; my steps are gone. . .
    Yes, it's a total loss."

Of course, they had no food to eat:
    No cheese, no fruit, no bread.
No one could shop for anything;
    "We're all locked in," they said.

They sat there then for ten whole days;
    They got quite pale and thin.
The butcher tried, the baker tried,
    But no one could get in.

Then father called the city hall,
    And they were kind enough
To send a helicopter out:
    It landed on the roof.

They didn't have to pay a cent,
    For it was "on the town."
The helicopter picked them up
    And brought them safely down.

Then Mother said, "Now we must build
    Some steps immediately."
But Father said, "I'm not so sure;
    Let's just sit back and see."

So that's the way they left it then,
    And it's still "on the town."
They use the helicopter now
    For going up and down.

And Father grins: "The steps, I say,
Were too old-fashioned anyway."

The Girl with Nylon Hair

Over the water of Saint Koedelare
Sat a young maiden with nylon hair,
Sat in a tower, imprisoned, alone,
Sat in a tower of stone.

Then a young fisherman came over there,
Over the water of Saint Koedelare.
Close to the tower he anchored near land,
There saw the maiden stand.

"Please come and join me, don't stand there and sigh!
Over the water together we'll fly!
Is there no stairway, no window pane?
Is there no silver chain?"

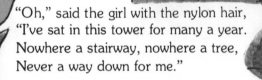

"Oh," said the girl with the nylon hair,
"I've sat in this tower for many a year.
Nowhere a stairway, nowhere a tree,
Never a way down for me."

Poor little prisoner! Years, months, and weeks,
Tears had been flowing down her pretty cheeks.
Trickling along down the tower of stone,
Dropping down, one by one.

Because so many big tears fell there,
Up rose the water of Saint Koedelare.
Up rose the boat to the window — fast!
They were together at last.

Off went the girl with the nylon hair,
Off with the fisherman, with him to fare
Over the waves and water, and then —
They never came back again.

35

Doll Party

In the land of Lolly Dolly
Stands the castle of a queen;
The doors are blue, the roof is red,
And all the towers are green.
Who is this queen? What does she do?
She is the queen of dollies;
She has a dimple in her chin
And plans the dolly follies.

Yes, every year she gives a ball
Which every doll attends —
A kind of boogie-woogie ball
For dollies and their friends.
Now you may think she didn't ask
Your dolls to come along
To dance the boogie-woogie-woo,
But wait! You may be wrong!

When you were lying in your bed,
What stopped at your front door?
A dolly bus with dolly flags,
And carpets on the floor.
From all the houses on your street
The dolls came running down
In pink or blue, in green or red —
The cutest dolls in town!

And all your dolls crept
  down the hall
To take the bus that night;
You didn't know
  that they had gone,
For you were sleeping tight.

Away they went! The bus was full!
They sneaked away from you,
As hand in hand or cheek to cheek
They sat there two by two.

The teddy bear sat up in front —
He took the driver's seat;
He drove at eighty miles an hour,
A-roaring down the street!
The queen of dolls was at the door,
Her dimple in her chin,
And as she greeted every doll,
She said, "Just walk right in."

And then they danced the boogie-woog —
That is a dolly dance —
The songs they sang were dolly songs
Which dollies sing in France.

They ate the dolly ice cream,
And they drank the dolly pop,
And ate the dolly pies and cakes
Until they thought they'd drop.

And so in Lolly Dolly Land
The dolls had lots of fun,
But finally the pretty queen
Said, "Put your coats back on."
The dolly ball was over then;
They all said, "What a night!"
And you — you didn't hear a thing,
For you were sleeping tight!

The Lady of Castle Van Karp

There once was a lady of Castle Van Karp
Who spent every day always playing her harp.
Her playing was lovely: Ring ding, dingle dee.
"But no one," she said, "ever listens to me."
She played all the classics, she played sonatinas,
And one day she called to her servant Marinus;
"Yes, Mam," said Marinus. "What is it? What is it?"
"Please ask the tall baron to come for a visit;
The colonel, the major, and Admiral Flem,
And tell them I'll play a fine concert for them."
Marinus went out — looking dapper and sharp —
And told them his mistress was playing the harp.

       The baron said, "Great,
       but I just made a date."
       The colonel — "Sublime!"
       but he didn't have time.
       The major would come
       if it only were drum.
       And Admiral Flem
       merely muttered, "Ahem."
Marinus went home and said, "What shall we do?
For no one, just no one will listen to you."

"Oh, dear," said the lady of Castle Van Karp,
"Forever just play by myself on my harp?
My lovely sonatas, my grand sonatinas
With no one to listen? Once more now, Marinus!
Go out on the street, go and knock at each door,
And try to get guests for my concert once more.
Just urge them to come — better try it again:
The butcher, the barber, professional men;
Go out and get started; I'll leave it to you —
You might ask the mayor and minister, too."
Marinus went out — looking dapper and sharp —
To tell them his mistress was playing the harp.

38

The butcher said, "Sweet,"
but he had to cut meat;
The mayor just knew
he had something to do.
The lawyers and doctors,
the town engineers
said, "Sorry, our work
is piled up to our ears."
Marinus went home and said, "What shall we do?
For no one, just no one will listen to you."

"Oh, dear," said the lady of Castle Van Karp,
"Will nobody listen to me and my harp?
Just go out once more now," she said to Marinus,
"And try to find someone who likes sonatinas."
He said to his lady, "Well, here in the house
There's one thing you'll find: you'll find many a mouse."
"Well, then," said the lady, "just let them come in,
And tell them to hurry; I want to begin."
She started to play: Ring ding, dingle dum. . .
As soon as she played, the mice started to come.
They sat on their haunches and danced on their toes,
They jumped on her harp, and ran over her clothes.

And when she had finished, then came the applause!
They all stood up straight as they clapped with their paws.
They shouted, "Bravo!" and "Hurray for the harp!"
And "Long live the lady of Castle Van Karp!"

39

Electric Blanket

My uncle and aunt
From Chillingwold
Are always suffering
From the cold.
They go to bed
While it's still light
And shake and shiver
Throughout the night.

Icy cold
Like winter weather
There they lie
In bed together.
Woolen mittens,
Woolen caps —
They wear all
Their winter wraps.
Water bottles
For their feet,
But they hardly
Feel the heat.
Hand in hand
They always lie,
Electric blanket
Turned up high.

The heat is set
At eighty-eight,
A fire is burning
On the grate.
The oven's on —
It doesn't matter —
They're still ice cold;
Their teeth still chatter.

My uncle and aunt
From Chillingwold
Are always suffering
From the cold.
Their son and daughter
Suffer, too,
Teeth achatter,
Fingers blue.
With chilly toes
All four they lie,
Electric blanket
Turned up high.

My uncle and aunt
From Chillingwold
Are always suffering
From the cold.
After hearing
The news and weather,
They all four go
To bed together:

Ice cold father,
Ice cold mother,
Ice cold sister,
Ice cold brother.
Some with mittens
Some with hat,
Also their dog
And their ice cold cat.
All six freezing,
There they lie —
Electric blanket
Turned up high.

They set it on TEN!
They set it on RED!

And still
they
lie
shivering
In
their
bed.

The Magic Wand

One day when Jimmy Jingaling was walking near the pond,
He had a very big surprise: he found a magic wand.
He walked back home to find his dad and try the magic word;
He said it: "HOCUS, POCUS, PIE! I wish you were a bird."
His mother looked at him aghast and cried, "What did you do?"
But Jim said, "HOCUS, POCUS," and she was a birdie, too.
So they flew out to find a tree, to whistle, and to tweet,
And Jimmy Jingaling went out to walk along the street.

He quickly changed three gentlemen into three big brown bears;
Some ladies who were walking there became two handsome mares.
Then Jimmy ran to school to see what changes he could make;
Of dear Miss Brown he made a mouse, of Mr. Blake, a cake.
He didn't change the boys and girls, with whom he liked to play —
Jerome and Kathy, Pete and Jack — he liked them just that way.
He only changed the grown-up folks; he walked through every street;
"I'll wave my wand," he said, "and change each grown-up whom I meet."

42

He changed the mayor of the town into a big red fox,
And Mrs. Green — the florist's wife — he changed her into phlox.
And all the children followed him — you should have heard them laugh
Whenever Jimmy made a duck, a peacock, or giraffe.
Then they would shout, "Hurrah, hurrah!" at each new mouse or fawn,
And after fourteen hours or so the grown-ups all were gone.
So now the children had their way: played cowboy in the park,
Played cops and robbers all day long until way after dark.

But strange enough, the cowboy games began to be a bore;
Now no one kept them neat and clean or kissed them anymore.
They all were very lonesome, but there wasn't much to do.
Their dads and moms were birds or bears or maybe caribou.
They sat down in a circle, and they all began to cry,
Till little Jimmy Jingaling said, "HOCUS, POCUS, PIE."
And then the grown-ups all came back, just as they were before!
The children cheered and clapped their hands — no one could wish for
    more!

They all came back, that is, but one: the teacher, Mr. Blake;
Yes, someone must have eaten him, for he had been a cake.

43

Circus Song

Go with the circus the whole world through—
That's what I would like to do!
To every land where the circus goes,
Appearing in all the evening shows,
London, Madrid, and Tokyo, too,
Go with the circus the whole world through.

Even if all
    They'd let me do
    Is set up chairs
    Or feed the bears,   But most of all — if you please —
    Or try to train   To be an artist on the trapeze.
    The lion's mane,   If you please,
    Or fill the boxes   On the trapeze!
    And tend the foxes.   On the trapeze!

Go with the circus the whole world through —
That's what I intend to do.
Go with the circus! What a ball!
Summer, winter, spring, and fall.
Brussels, Berlin, and Bali, too,
Go with the circus the whole world through.

Even if only
    To set up tents
    For the elephants,
    Or hold the sticks   But most of all — if you please —
    For the poodle's tricks,   Up in the air on the high trapeze!
    Or comb the curls   If you please,
    Of the dancing girls.   On the trapeze!
                      On the trapeze!

Summer Evening

I'm lying in bed
but the sun is still up
and my sisters have gone for a ride
I have to stay here
they made that quite clear
while everyone else is outside

a radio's playing
my brother is saying
that he's going out to play ball
they're watching TV
and drinking their tea
and I don't feel sleepy at all

I'm lying in bed
don't get up, Mother said,
the clock has already struck eight
I'm hungry for cake
or a chocolate milk shake
but I don't dare to ask — it's too late

I'm trying to sleep
I'm counting my sheep
but the sun is still shining too bright
I don't think it's fair
that they're playing out there
and I'm here alone every night

What is That, Mrs. Van Teller?

"What is that, Mrs. Van Teller?
Are those bears down in your cellar?
Big brown bears down in your cellar, actually?
Now if you were keeping monkeys,
Or if they were even donkeys,
But to keep brown bears, and real ones! Oh, dear me!"

"Now look here once, Mr. Fishun,
Must I ask for your permission?
Mind your own affairs I tell you, just don't touch!
I advise you not to bother,
For these bears came from my father,
And I love each of the seven very much!"

"Think I'm scared?" said Mr. Fishun,
"Why I'll call the town commission!
They'll send out a big policeman with a gun!"
Then the lady got quite vicious:
"If you want to get officious,
I'll send all my bears right at you on the run!

I invite you to come near them
So that you can really hear them":
"Grr grr," said the bears with all their might.
"Do you hear that, Mr. Fishun!
Must I still ask your permission?"
"Oh, well, no, Mrs. Van Teller, that's all right.

Well good day, my charming lady,
My, your lawn is nice and shady!
May your bears bring many pleasures to your life!"
"Well so long then, Mr. Fishun,
Come again — with my permission —
And be sure to give my greetings to your wife!"
            Grrr! Grr!

On the Green

Four tall poplars on the green
tallest trees I've ever seen
winds are whistling through them there
and the sun shines on their hair
and they rustle as they sing
for the bunnies in the spring
for the flowers who nod and smell
for the weeds they sing as well
for the bees and for the birds
whispering their soothing words
I feel sorry for the folks who haven't seen
those popular old poplars on the green.

When the sparrows fly in fright
from the stormy clouds at night
when the skies are dark and gray
and the robins hide away
when a storm is threatening
then the poplars start to sing
don't be frightened little flower
this is just a little shower
don't be worried little bunny
it will soon be bright and sunny
little sparrows don't start crying
robin redbreast keep on flying
that's the way the poplars sing
when it's stormy in the spring
It never does last long, as we have seen,
say the popular old poplars on the green.

Late at Night

As soon as it gets dark out, and the moon begins to shine,
The people in the houses draw their curtains and their blinds.
And then the big fat carpenter and Mrs. Taylor, too,
All go to sleep just like the cat and all her kittens do.
And all the colts fall fast asleep, each one beside his mother,
And all the little pigs, and Mr. Farmer and his brother.
The little calves, the little lambs, and even the big dog,
And all the little children lie there sleeping like a log.
And when the hens are sleeping, and the fishes in the streams,
A little man comes running with his basket full of dreams.

As soon as they start dreaming, all the fishes think they're whales;
The carpenter starts counting all his hammers and his nails.
And Mrs. Taylor dreams that she is taking cooking courses,
And all the little colts that they are finally big horses.
The children dream of ice cream, and the hens about their eggs,
And all the little calves that they have very sturdy legs.
Yes, just at ten, when all the fish are sleeping in their streams,
That little man comes running with his basket full of dreams.

He has just one left over, made of yellow, pink, and blue,
And when you fall asleep tonight, that dream will be for you.

49

The Goat of Dr. Pottle

The goat of Dr. Pottle
is quite a different model
is quite a different thing
from the goat of Dr. Ding,
from the goat of Dr. Ding,
from the goat of Dr. Dingalingaling.

Doctor Pottle feels quite bad
and it gets him very mad.
He gets cross with everything,
for the goat of Dr. Ding
is a very different thing
from the goat he leads about.
All the people stand and shout,
"Isn't it a crazy thing
that the goat of Dr. Pottle
is such a very different model
from the goat of Dr. Ding,
from the goat of Dr. Ding,
from the goat of Dr. Dingalingaling!"

Dr. Ding across the way
Gets just as angry every day.
He mutters in a terrible tirade:
"I guess we just had better make a trade.
Let's do it *now*," says Dr. Ding,

Pottle says, "The very thing!"
They struck the bargain right away
and traded goats that very day.
But it hasn't helped at all!
You still hear the people call,
All the folks just stand and say,
"Isn't it a crazy thing
That the goat of Dr. Pottle
is such a *very* different model
from the goat of Dr. Ding,
from the goat of Dr. Ding,
from the goat of Dr. Dingalingaling!"

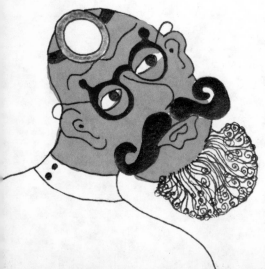

Johanna Cracklebone

This is Johanna Cracklebone:
She does go out, but *not* alone.
Her bulldog always goes along;
They both look threatening and strong.
Her bulldog's name is Jim Van Dyke;
The dog and she look just alike!

The neighbors whom they chance to meet
Are always quick to cross the street.
The people — big and small alike —
Are terrified to meet Van Dyke.
He paws the ground and looks for fights,
He growls at people, and he bites.

And you should see the awful fuss
When dog and mistress ride the bus!
As soon as they step through the door,
Some passengers faint on the floor.
The others scream, "He's biting us!"
And push each other off the bus.
Then just Johanna and Van Dyke
Are on the bus — just what they like.

Since she won't leave him in the lurch,
She also takes her dog to church.
Then you should see the sudden rush:
The people jump and run and push.
It's evident that they don't like
Johanna, or her dog Van Dyke.
Soon he and grim Miss Cracklebone
Are sitting in the church alone.

And then, although it broke the rule,
Johanna took her dog to school.
But when they walked into room three,
The lessons stopped immediately.
The children jumped and pushed and cried,
And through the halls they rushed outside.
The teacher stood there like a dunce
Until they called an ambulance.
And soon again Miss Cracklebone
Was sitting with her dog alone.

This was too much! This had to stop!
They called the council and a cop.
They searched around for this and that
Until they found an acrobat:
"This is the man we will engage
To lock them both into a cage."
He caught them; there they sit alone —
Van Dyke and his Miss Cracklebone!

You'll see them both in church next week,
But in their cage — both mild and meek.
At school they can't do any wrong
Because their cage is good and strong.
Johanna is no longer hated;
Van Dyke is getting educated!
Their study habits can't be beat,
And, best of all, they both look sweet!

51

Henderson of Lexington

Oh, hello there, Miss Van Hews,
Have you heard the latest news?
Henderson
Of Lexington
Left the kitchen faucet run.
For hours and hours, just think,
It trickled from the sink.
It covered the whole floor
And some say even more!
Too bad, too bad, too bad!
How sad, how sad, how sad!

    Why, good morning, Mrs. Fleer,
    I have news you ought to hear:
    Henderson
    Of Lexington
    Left the kitchen faucet run.
    Seven days, from dawn till dark!
    The house is floating like an ark!
    Imagine what a feeling —
    The tables hit the ceiling!

Morning, Mrs. Ferlinghetti,
Have you heard the news already?
Henderson
Of Lexington
Left the kitchen faucet run.
Seven weeks without a stop!
All the streets are covered up!
The neighbors were annoyed —
Their cars were all destroyed!

Hi there, Mrs. Vander Zee,
What a big catastrophe!
Henderson
Of Lexington
Left the kitchen faucet run.

Seven months he left it on!
Now the town's completely gone.
Just imagine what they said:
EVERYONE IS DEAD!

But look!
Who's coming on the run?
Henderson
Of Lexington!
Just what happened, Henderson,
When you left the faucet run?
Oh, he said, it wasn't long;
People make it far too strong!
On the floor
One little splash —
Wiped it up
Like a flash!
Just one minute, it was done,
That was all, said Henderson.

Sad and
        disappointed then,
The ladies
        all
            went home
                    again.

The Best Child

The best child I have ever known
Was Peter Henry Hagelstone.
He always, always wiped his feet
And kept the house and garden neat.
At night — unasked — he went to bed
And always ate his meat and bread;
He even ate his spinach, too,
And asked for harder work to do!
He never said a dirty word —
At least not one you ever heard.
He did not kick, he was not bold,
He always did as he was told.
No smears of chocolate on his cheeks;
He kept one shirt clean four whole weeks!
He wore one coat — so it appears —
Without a patch for five whole years.

When he grew up, he thought he'd marry
A lady named Miss Blossomberry.
They have six children — all a fright —
Who kick and scream both day and night.
They never, never wipe their feet
Nor finish up their bread and meat.
They play right in the muddy gutter,
They cry and stamp, they scowl and mutter.
They stain their clothes in scores of places,
They pull the most horrendous faces,
Till Peter Henry Hagelstone
Can only wring his hands and moan!
Which goes to show, I'm sad to say,
That goodness doesn't always pay!

Is Kittily-Puss a Cat?

The story of Kittily-Puss, my dears,
    Is very, very sad!
His father and mother, his uncle and aunt
    Are feeling very bad.
They look him over from every side —
    The top, the front, the back —
They sniff around and then they say,
    "He must be out of whack."
He has two kitten ears, it's true,
    He has a kitten nose,
Two kitten eyes, a kitten tail,
    And even kitten toes.
He has a kind of kitten smell —
    They seem quite sure of that —
But still they say that Kittily-Puss
    Is really not a cat.

His brothers and his sisters say,
    "But what's the matter, Dad?"
And Daddy answers, "Not so loud!
    It's shameful, and it's sad!
This cat's a coward! Scared of mice!"
    Just then his mother cries,
"Look, look! The mice are after him!"
    And up a tree he flies.
His uncle and his auntie, too,
    Say, "Kittily, we're ashamed of you!"

So all of Kittily's family
    Sit sadly in the house,
For they all know that no real cat
    Is frightened by a mouse.
His manners just don't suit a cat —
    And what in the world can you do about that?

The Ducks

There once were some ducks on a pond by a jetty
Who said, "Johnny fed us so often already;
Let's turn it around now; let's do it this way:
We ducks will go out to feed Johnny today."

So one bought some butter, another an egg—
Each one had a grocery bag on his leg—
They bought some fresh oranges, some butter and jam,
And then off to Johnny's house—all on the tram.

As Johnny came out with his crumbs on a plate,
He saw the three ducks standing there at the gate.
"Hi, Johnny," they said, "just go right back inside;
We're going to feed you—we're turning the tide."

So Johnny sat down on his chair to be fed;
The ducks fluttered round him—one perched on his head!
They fed him his toast and his cereal, too,
And one said, "Here, Johnny! Some orange juice for you!"

"Well, well," said the ducks, "this is ducky to do:
You came to feed us, and now we're feeding you!"
And then they called out as they walked through the gate,
"Tomorrow it's your turn; be sure you're not late."

Calm, Calm

One day a calm, calm lady
And a man as calm as she
Went fishing in a little boat
Out on a calm, calm sea.

They caught three calm, calm fishes
And brought them back to the house,
Where they had some calm, calm chickens
And also a calm, calm mouse.

They did some calm, calm reading —
The book was slow and mild —
And after a little time had passed,
They had a calm, calm child.

And when that child got sleepy,
" 'Night, Pop, 'night, Mom," he said,
And fourteen calm, calm angels
Carried him off to bed.

57

The Clean Queen

"Now get to work! Now get to work!"
An order from the Queen!
"I see some dust out on the street
And mud on the policemen's feet!
I want things nice and clean!"

Of course, the Queen is very fair,
But she believes in order!
So every lawn and every square
Must first be laundered everywhere,
Then vacuumed round the border!

The cows all have to bathe each day
To make them sanitary,
And every tree along the way
Is polished with a fragrant spray
To keep things nice and airy!

So everything looks neat and clean,
No dirt allowed at all!
Though lots of little dogs are seen,
On every street a dog latrine
Is built into the wall!

Each night the Queen deserts the ball
To look around a bit.
She wipes her finger down each wall,
And if there's any dust at all,
She really throws a fit!

If anyone drops just one hair
On any sidewalk anywhere,
He is beheaded on the spot,
For that annoys the Queen a lot!
Yes, she's a very friendly queen,
But just a trifle OVER clean!

58

A-Nibble No, A-Nibble Nice

A-nibble no, a-nibble nice,
A fine old pair of friendly mice
Are living in the upstairs hall
Behind the paper on the wall.

Their daughter's wedding was today;
She married a fine mouse, they say,
So handsome as he spoke his vow —
They're living in the bookcase now.

Then Mother Mouse said, through her tears,
"The nicest wedding day in years!
Our daughter looked so dignified;
She really made a darling bride."

And Father Mouse, who looked so glum,
Said, "I could hardly eat a crumb!
I cried because she looked so sweet,
And when I cry, I just can't eat.
I did feel bad, but now I think
That we should have a little drink.
They're just as happy as can be,
So cut a piece of cheese for me.
And don't forget," he said to Mother,
"That you and I still have each other."

A-nibble no, a-nibble nice,
A fine old pair of friendly mice
Are living in the upstairs hall
Behind the paper on the wall.

The Proud Little Light

There was a glowing Christmas tree
	with a hundred thousand lights;
The children stood around and sang
	of silent, holy nights.

One of the lights was wondering
	if he was needed there;
The room was really bright enough
	with lots of lights to spare.

"I'll fly out in the dark," he said,
	"to shine out in the snow."
So through the open window then
	the children saw him go.

"Look, look! There flies a light," they cried,
	"up there among the trees.
Let's catch him quick," but he was gone,
	asailing on the breeze.

He flew across the fields and woods,
    he flew and flew so far
That people said, "Why, this is rare!
    We see a brand new star!"

The little light felt very proud;
    he liked to sail about.
"Look at me shine," he said, "so bright
    I never will go out!"

But then a stormy wind arose
    with icy sleet and snow;
The little light began to fall —
    the people saw him go.

"Oh, look, we see a falling star,
    and this is what we'll do:
We'll make a wish, for falling stars
    make every wish come true.

And since today is Christmas day,
    we'll wish for peace at last!
We've never seen a star that fell
    down to the earth so fast."

The people all felt very glad;
    they all felt warm inside,
And all of them began to work:
    "We must work hard," they cried,

"So that the peace for which we wished
    will really come about."
As for the star, he fell to earth,
    and glowed, and faded out.

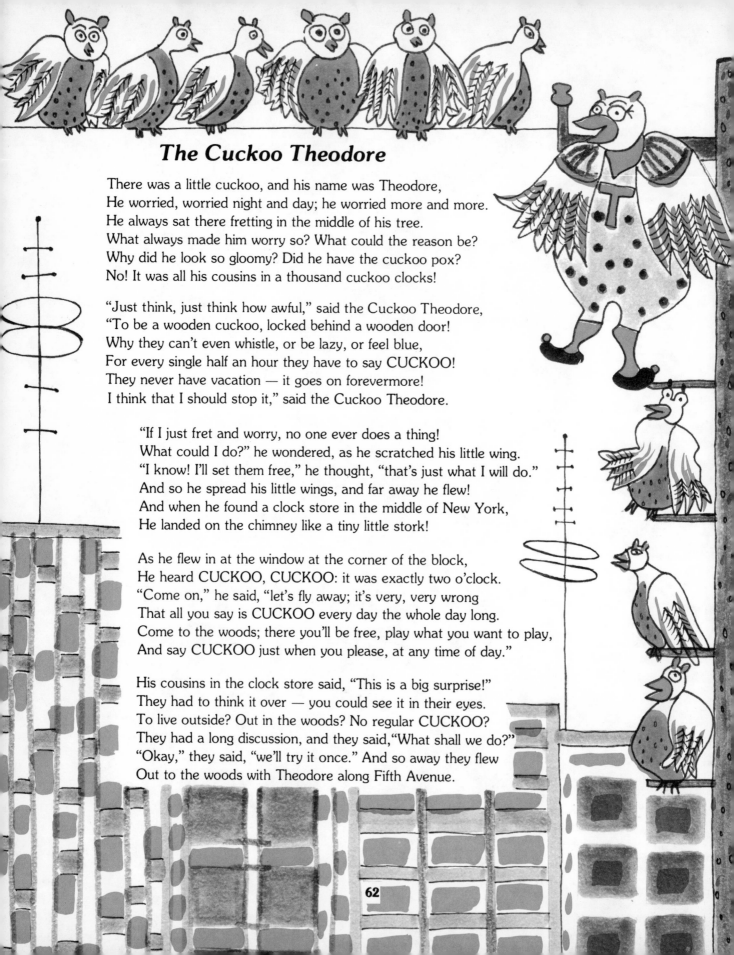

The Cuckoo Theodore

There was a little cuckoo, and his name was Theodore,
He worried, worried night and day; he worried more and more.
He always sat there fretting in the middle of his tree.
What always made him worry so? What could the reason be?
Why did he look so gloomy? Did he have the cuckoo pox?
No! It was all his cousins in a thousand cuckoo clocks!

"Just think, just think how awful," said the Cuckoo Theodore,
"To be a wooden cuckoo, locked behind a wooden door!
Why they can't even whistle, or be lazy, or feel blue,
For every single half an hour they have to say CUCKOO!
They never have vacation — it goes on forevermore!
I think that I should stop it," said the Cuckoo Theodore.

"If I just fret and worry, no one ever does a thing!
What could I do?" he wondered, as he scratched his little wing.
"I know! I'll set them free," he thought, "that's just what I will do."
And so he spread his little wings, and far away he flew!
And when he found a clock store in the middle of New York,
He landed on the chimney like a tiny little stork!

As he flew in at the window at the corner of the block,
He heard CUCKOO, CUCKOO: it was exactly two o'clock.
"Come on," he said, "let's fly away; it's very, very wrong
That all you say is CUCKOO every day the whole day long.
Come to the woods; there you'll be free, play what you want to play,
And say CUCKOO just when you please, at any time of day."

His cousins in the clock store said, "This is a big surprise!"
They had to think it over — you could see it in their eyes.
To live outside? Out in the woods? No regular CUCKOO?
They had a long discussion, and they said, "What shall we do?"
"Okay," they said, "we'll try it once." And so away they flew
Out to the woods with Theodore along Fifth Avenue.

62